ESSENTIAL ELEMENTS®

GUITAR ENSEMBLES

IRISH JIGS & REELS

CONTENTS

Arrangements by Mark Phillips

ISBN 978-1-4803-9895-5

HAL•LEONARD®
CORPORATION

7777 W. BLUEMOUND RD. P.O. BOX 13819 MILWAUKEE, WI 53213

In Australia Contact:
Hal Leonard Australia Pty. Ltd.
4 Lentara Court
Cheltenham, Victoria, 3192 Australia
Email: ausadmin@halleonard.com.au

Visit Hal Leonard Online at
www.halleonard.com

DROWSY MAGGIE

Traditional

HANGMAN'S REEL

Traditional

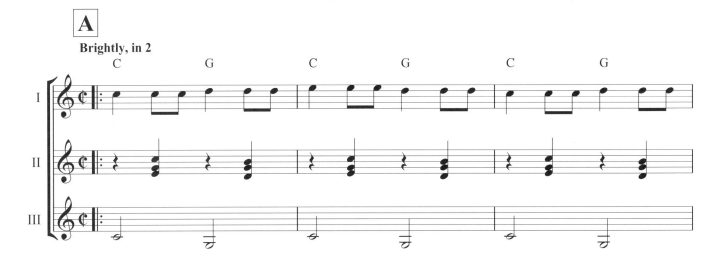

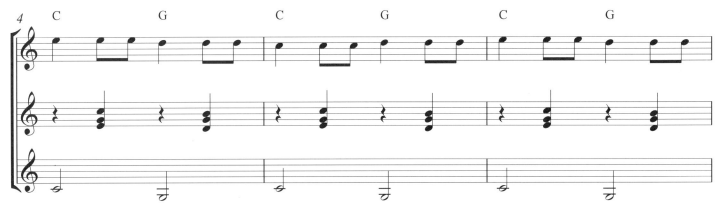

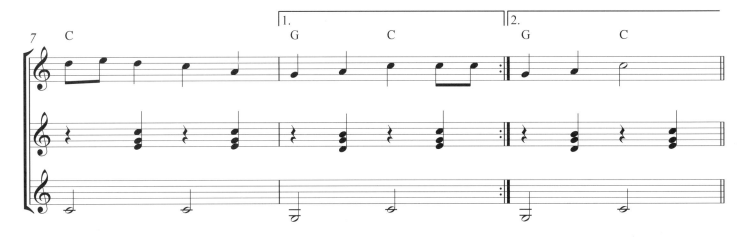

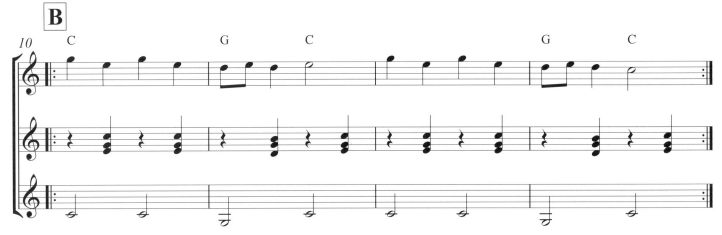

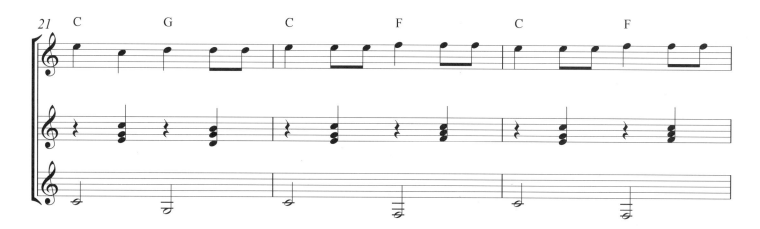

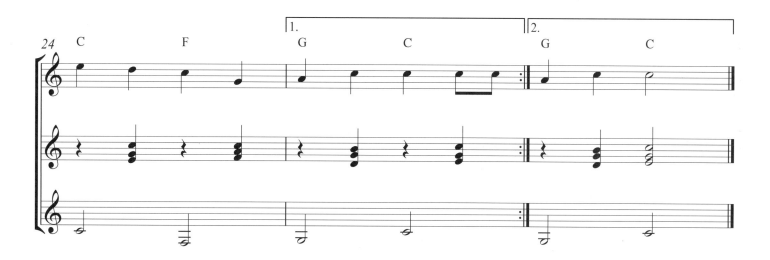

THE IRISH WASHERWOMAN

Irish Folksong

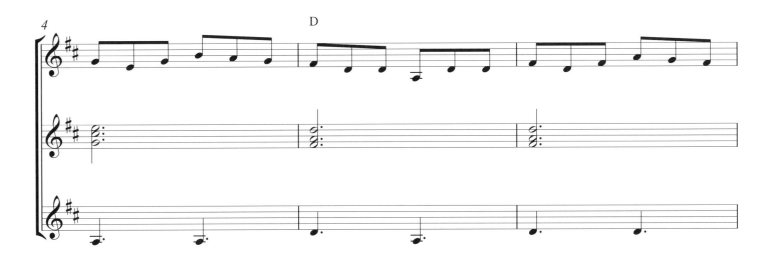

B

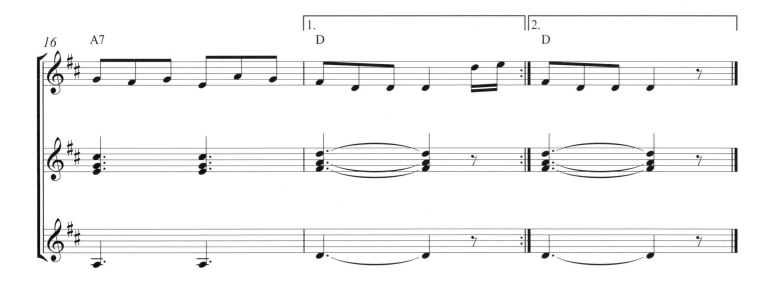

THE JIG OF SLURS

Traditional

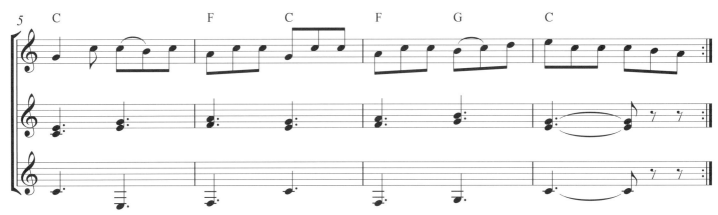

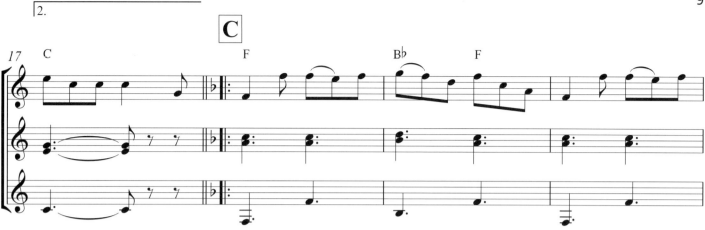

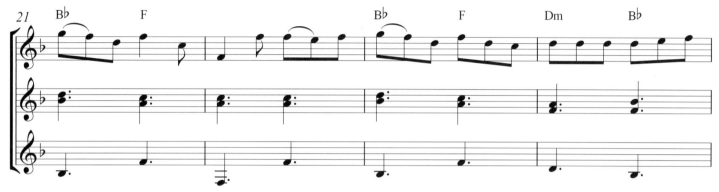

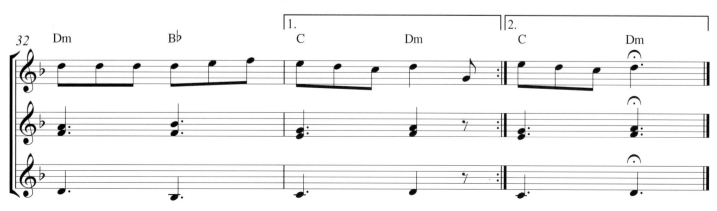

THE KESH JIG

Traditional Irish

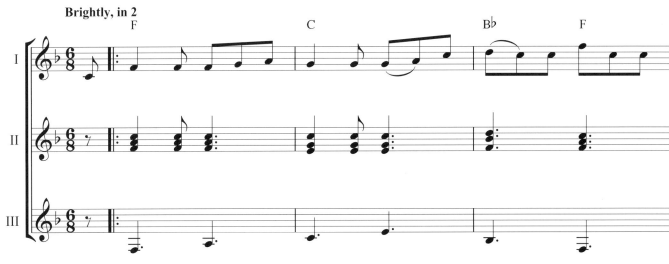

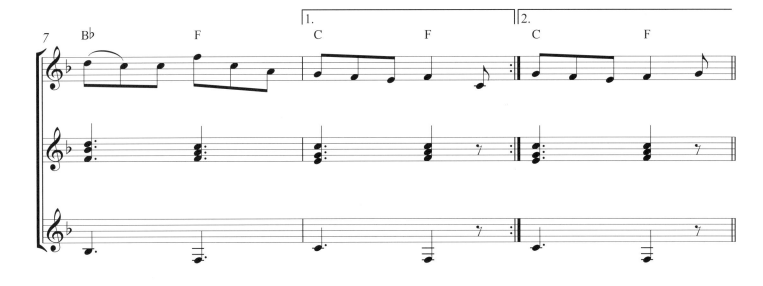

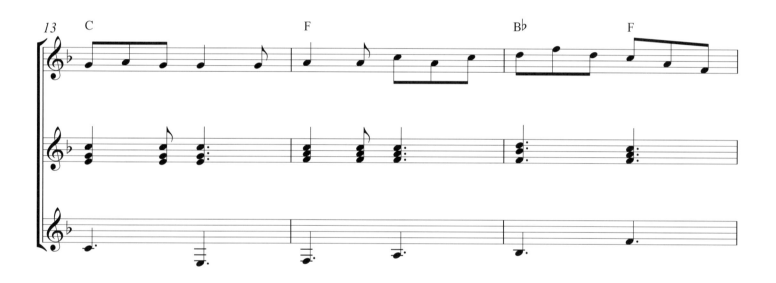

THE LITTLE BEGGARMAN

Traditional Irish Folk Song

MOLLY ON THE SHORE

By Percy Aldridge Grainger

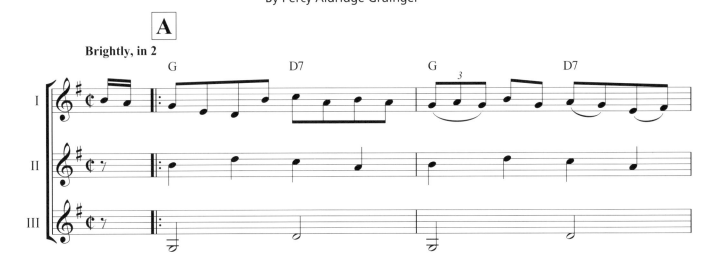

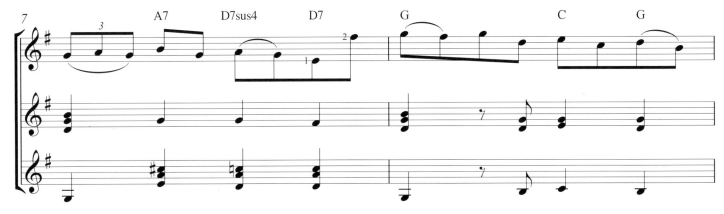

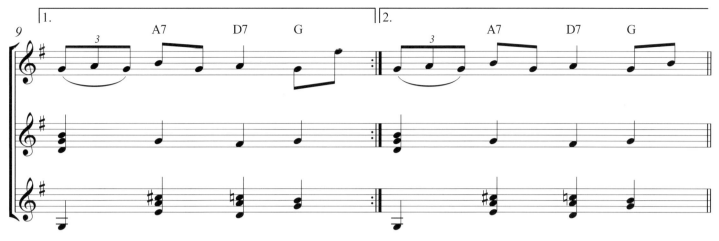

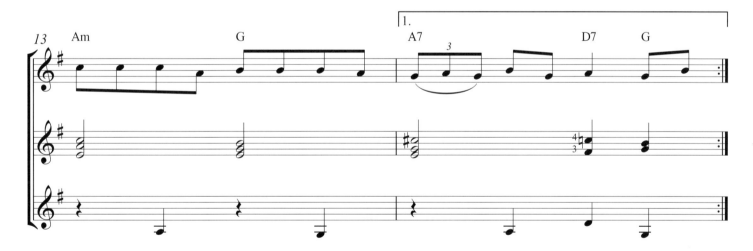

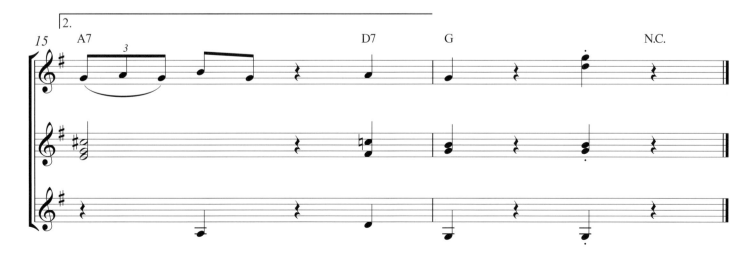

MORRISON'S JIG

Traditional Irish Folk Song

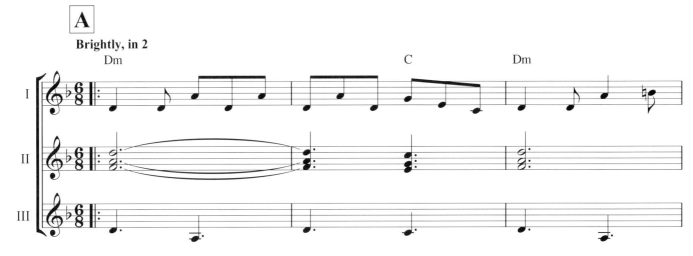

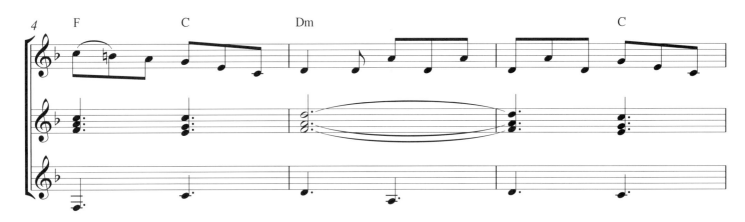

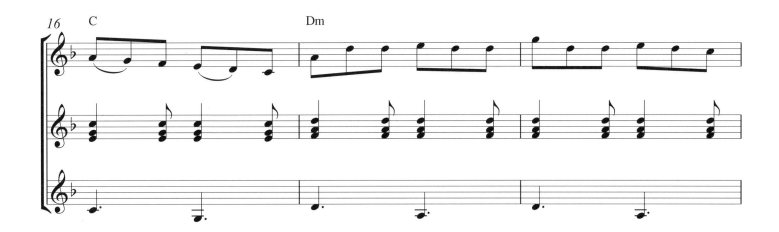

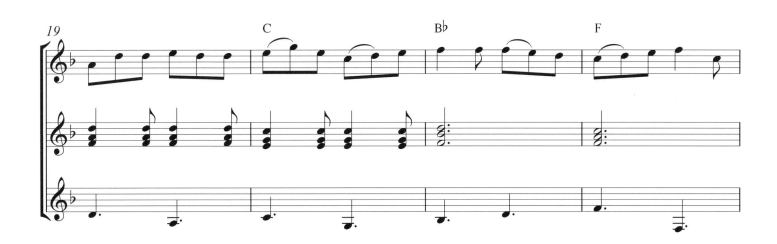

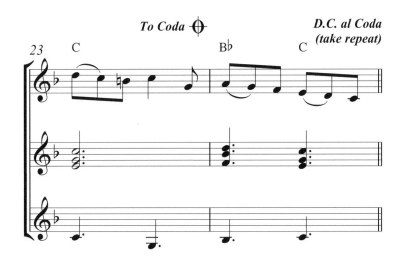

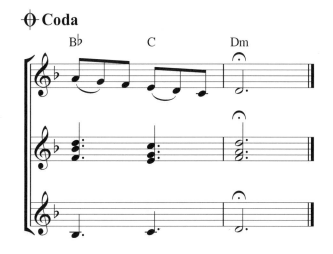

SHEEHAN'S REEL

Traditional

SHIPS ARE SAILING

Traditional Irish Reel

A

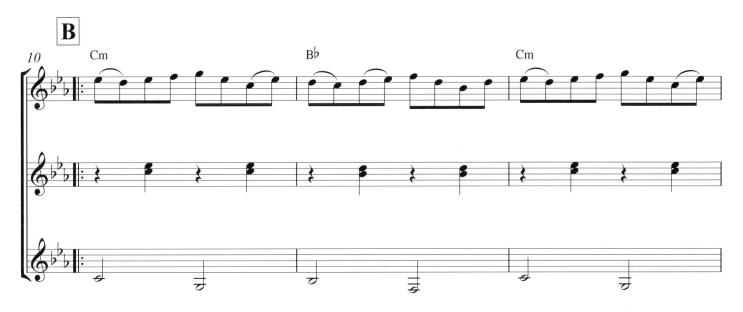

STAR OF MUNSTER

Traditional Irish

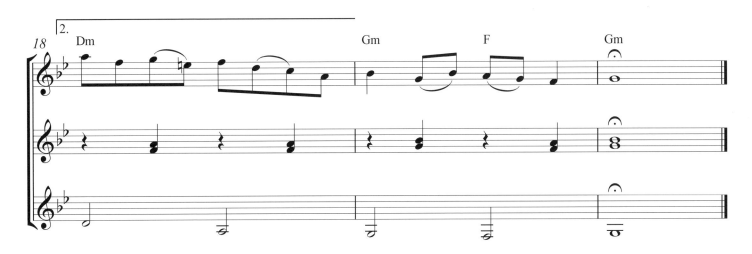

SWALLOWTAIL JIG

Traditional Irish Jig

B

TARBOULTON REEL

Traditional

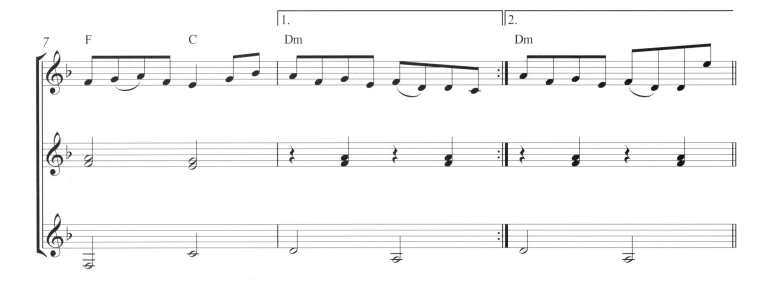

TEMPERENCE REEL
(Temperance Reel)
Traditional

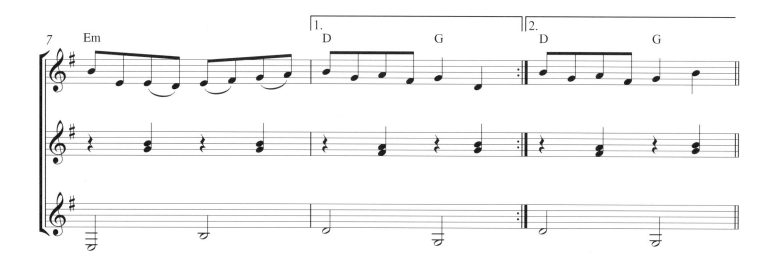

ESSENTIAL ELEMENTS FOR GUITAR

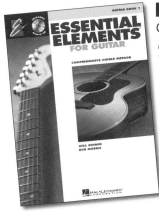

BOOK 1

Comprehensive Guitar Method
by Will Schmid and Bob Morris

Take your guitar teaching to a new level! With the time-tested classroom teaching methods of Will Schmid and Bob Morris, popular songs in a variety of styles, and quality demonstration and backing tracks on the accompanying CD, *Essential Elements for Guitar* is a staple of guitar teachers' instruction – and helps beginning guitar students off to a great start.

This method has been designed to meet the National Standards for Music Education, with features such as cross-curricular activities, quizzes, multicultural songs, basic improvisation and more. Concepts covered in Book 1 include: getting started; basic music theory; guitar chords; notes on each string; music history; ensemble playing; performance spotlights; and much more!

Songs used in Book 1 include such hits as: Dust in the Wind • Eleanor Rigby • Every Breath You Take • Hey Jude • Hound Dog • Let It Be • Ode to Joy • Rock Around the Clock • Stand by Me • Surfin' USA • Sweet Home Chicago • This Land Is Your Land • You Really Got Me • and more!

00862639 Book/CD Pack $17.99
00001173 Book Only $9.99

BOOK 2

Bob Morris

Essential Elements for Guitar, Book 2 is a continuation of the concepts and skills taught in Book 1 and includes all of its popular features as well – great songs in a variety of styles, a high-quality audio CD with demonstration and backing tracks, quizzes, music history, music theory, and much more. Concepts taught in Book 2 include: Playing melodically in positions up the neck; Playing movable chord shapes up the neck; Playing scales and extended chords in different keys; More right-hand studies – fingerpicking and pick style; Improvisation in positions up the neck; Studying different styles through great song selections; and more!

00865010 Book/CD Pack $17.99
00120873 Book Only $10.99

DAILY GUITAR WARM-UPS

by Tom Kolb

Mid-Beginner to Late Intermediate

This book contains a wide variety of exercises to help get your hands in top playing shape. It addresses the basic elements of guitar warm-ups by category: stretches and pre-playing coordination exercises, picking exercises, right and left-hand synchronization, and rhythm guitar warm-ups.

00865004 Book/CD Pack $9.99

Essential Elements Guitar Ensembles

The songs in the Essential Elements Guitar Ensemble series are playable by three or more guitars. Each arrangement features the melody, a harmony part, and bass line in standard notation along with chord symbols. For groups with more than three or four guitars, the parts can be doubled. This series is perfect for classroom guitar ensembles or other group guitar settings.

J.S. BACH
00123103 Early Intermediate Level.................................$9.99

THE BEATLES
00865008 Early Intermediate Level.................................$9.99

BOSSA NOVA
00865006 Intermediate/Advanced Level......................$9.99

CHRISTMAS CLASSICS
00865015 Mid-Intermediate Level $9.99

CHRISTMAS SONGS
00001136 Mid-Beginner Level $9.95

CLASSICAL THEMES
00865005 Late Beginner Level..$9.99

DISNEY SONGS
00865014 Early Intermediate Level.................................$9.99

EASY POP SONGS
00865011 Mid-Beginner Level $9.99

DUKE ELLINGTON
00865009 Mid-Intermediate Level $9.99

GREAT THEMES
00865012 Mid-Intermediate Level $9.99

JIMI HENDRIX
00865013 Mid-Intermediate Level $9.99

JAZZ BALLADS
00865002 Early Intermediate Level..............................$9.99

JAZZ STANDARDS
00865007 Mid-Intermediate Level $9.99

POP HITS
00001128 Late Beginner Level.......................................$9.99

ROCK CLASSICS
00865001 Late Beginner Level.......................................$9.95

ROCK INSTRUMENTALS
00123102 Mid-Intermediate Level $9.99

TOP HITS
00130606 Early Intermediate Level................................$9.99

Flash Cards

96 CARDS FOR BEGINNING GUITAR
00865000...$9.99

Essential Elements Guitar Songs

The books in the Essential Elements Guitar Songs series feature popular songs specially selected for the practice of specific guitar chord types. Each book includes eight great songs and a CD with fantastic sounding play-along tracks. Practice at any tempo with the included Amazing Slow Downer software!

POWER CHORD ROCK
Mid-Beginner Level
00001139 Book/CD Pack $12.99

OPEN CHORD ROCK
Mid-Beginner Level
00001138 Book/CD Pack $12.99

BARRE CHORD ROCK
Late Beginner Level
00001137 Book/CD Pack $12.99

FOR MORE INFORMATION, SEE YOUR LOCAL MUSIC DEALER,
OR WRITE TO:

HAL•LEONARD®
CORPORATION
7777 W. BLUEMOUND RD. P.O. BOX 13819 MILWAUKEE, WI 53213

Prices, contents, and availability subject to change without notice.

This series will help you play your favorite songs quickly and easily. Just follow the tab and listen to the audio to the hear how the guitar should sound, and then play along using the separate backing tracks. Mac or PC users can also slow down the tempo without changing pitch by using the CD in their computer. The melody and lyrics are included in the book so that you can sing or simply follow along.

INCLUDES TAB

VOL. 1 – ROCK	00699570 / $16.99	
VOL. 2 – ACOUSTIC	00699569 / $16.95	
VOL. 3 – HARD ROCK	00699573 / $16.95	
VOL. 4 – POP/ROCK	00699571 / $16.99	
VOL. 5 – MODERN ROCK	00699574 / $16.99	
VOL. 6 – '90S ROCK	00699572 / $16.99	
VOL. 7 – BLUES	00699575 / $16.95	
VOL. 8 – ROCK	00699585 / $14.99	
VOL. 10 – ACOUSTIC	00699586 / $16.95	
VOL. 11 – EARLY ROCK	00699579 / $14.95	
VOL. 12 – POP/ROCK	00699587 / $14.95	
VOL. 13 – FOLK ROCK	00699581 / $15.99	
VOL. 14 – BLUES ROCK	00699582 / $16.95	
VOL. 15 – R&B	00699583 / $16.99	
VOL. 16 – JAZZ	00699584 / $15.95	
VOL. 17 – COUNTRY	00699588 / $15.95	
VOL. 18 – ACOUSTIC ROCK	00699577 / $15.95	
VOL. 19 – SOUL	00699578 / $14.99	
VOL. 20 – ROCKABILLY	00699580 / $14.95	
VOL. 21 – YULETIDE	00699602 / $14.95	
VOL. 22 – CHRISTMAS	00699600 / $15.95	
VOL. 23 – SURF	00699635 / $14.95	
VOL. 24 – ERIC CLAPTON	00699649 / $17.99	
VOL. 25 – LENNON & MCCARTNEY	00699642 / $16.99	
VOL. 26 – ELVIS PRESLEY	00699643 / $14.95	
VOL. 27 – DAVID LEE ROTH	00699645 / $16.95	
VOL. 28 – GREG KOCH	00699646 / $14.95	
VOL. 29 – BOB SEGER	00699647 / $15.99	
VOL. 30 – KISS	00699644 / $16.99	
VOL. 31 – CHRISTMAS HITS	00699652 / $14.95	
VOL. 32 – THE OFFSPRING	00699653 / $14.95	
VOL. 33 – ACOUSTIC CLASSICS	00699656 / $16.95	
VOL. 34 – CLASSIC ROCK	00699658 / $16.95	
VOL. 35 – HAIR METAL	00699660 / $16.95	
VOL. 36 – SOUTHERN ROCK	00699661 / $16.95	
VOL. 37 – ACOUSTIC UNPLUGGED	00699662 / $22.99	
VOL. 38 – BLUES	00699663 / $16.95	
VOL. 39 – '80S METAL	00699664 / $16.99	
VOL. 40 – INCUBUS	00699668 / $17.95	
VOL. 41 – ERIC CLAPTON	00699669 / $16.95	
VOL. 42 – 2000S ROCK	00699670 / $16.99	
VOL. 43 – LYNYRD SKYNYRD	00699681 / $17.95	
VOL. 44 – JAZZ	00699689 / $14.99	
VOL. 45 – TV THEMES	00699718 / $14.95	
VOL. 46 – MAINSTREAM ROCK	00699722 / $16.95	
VOL. 47 – HENDRIX SMASH HITS	00699723 / $19.95	
VOL. 48 – AEROSMITH CLASSICS	00699724 / $17.99	
VOL. 49 – STEVIE RAY VAUGHAN	00699725 / $17.99	
VOL. 50 – VAN HALEN 1978-1984	00110269 / $17.99	
VOL. 51 – ALTERNATIVE '90S	00699727 / $14.99	
VOL. 52 – FUNK	00699728 / $14.95	
VOL. 53 – DISCO	00699729 / $14.99	
VOL. 54 – HEAVY METAL	00699730 / $14.95	
VOL. 55 – POP METAL	00699731 / $14.95	
VOL. 56 – FOO FIGHTERS	00699749 / $15.99	
VOL. 58 – BLINK-182	00699772 / $14.95	
VOL. 59 – CHET ATKINS	00702347 / $16.99	
VOL. 60 – 3 DOORS DOWN	00699774 / $14.95	
VOL. 61 – SLIPKNOT	00699775 / $16.99	
VOL. 62 – CHRISTMAS CAROLS	00699798 / $12.95	
VOL. 63 – CREEDENCE CLEARWATER REVIVAL	00699802 / $16.99	

VOL. 64 – THE ULTIMATE OZZY OSBOURNE	00699803 / $16.99	
VOL. 66 – THE ROLLING STONES	00699807 / $16.95	
VOL. 67 – BLACK SABBATH	00699808 / $16.99	
VOL. 68 – PINK FLOYD – DARK SIDE OF THE MOON	00699809 / $16.99	
VOL. 69 – ACOUSTIC FAVORITES	00699810 / $14.95	
VOL. 70 – OZZY OSBOURNE	00699805 / $16.99	
VOL. 71 – CHRISTIAN ROCK	00699824 / $14.95	
VOL. 73 – BLUESY ROCK	00699829 / $16.99	
VOL. 75 – TOM PETTY	00699882 / $16.99	
VOL. 76 – COUNTRY HITS	00699884 / $14.95	
VOL. 77 – BLUEGRASS	00699910 / $14.99	
VOL. 78 – NIRVANA	00700132 / $16.99	
VOL. 79 – NEIL YOUNG	00700133 / $24.99	
VOL. 80 – ACOUSTIC ANTHOLOGY	00700175 / $19.95	
VOL. 81 – ROCK ANTHOLOGY	00700176 / $22.99	
VOL. 82 – EASY SONGS	00700177 / $12.99	
VOL. 83 – THREE CHORD SONGS	00700178 / $16.99	
VOL. 84 – STEELY DAN	00700200 / $16.99	
VOL. 85 – THE POLICE	00700269 / $16.99	
VOL. 86 – BOSTON	00700465 / $16.99	
VOL. 87 – ACOUSTIC WOMEN	00700763 / $14.99	
VOL. 88 – GRUNGE	00700467 / $16.99	
VOL. 89 – REGGAE	00700468 / $15.99	
VOL. 90 – CLASSICAL POP	00700469 / $14.99	
VOL. 91 – BLUES INSTRUMENTALS	00700505 / $14.99	
VOL. 92 – EARLY ROCK INSTRUMENTALS	00700506 / $14.99	
VOL. 93 – ROCK INSTRUMENTALS	00700507 / $16.99	
VOL. 94 – SLOW BLUES	00700508 / $16.99	
VOL. 95 – BLUES CLASSICS	00700509 / $14.99	
VOL. 96 – THIRD DAY	00700560 / $14.95	
VOL. 97 – ROCK BAND	00700703 / $14.99	
VOL. 99 – ZZ TOP	00700762 / $16.99	
VOL. 100 – B.B. KING	00700466 / $16.99	
VOL. 101 – SONGS FOR BEGINNERS	00701917 / $14.99	
VOL. 102 – CLASSIC PUNK	00700769 / $14.99	
VOL. 103 – SWITCHFOOT	00700773 / $16.99	
VOL. 104 – DUANE ALLMAN	00700846 / $16.99	
VOL. 105 – LATIN	00700939 / $16.99	
VOL. 106 – WEEZER	00700958 / $14.99	
VOL. 107 – CREAM	00701069 / $16.99	
VOL. 108 – THE WHO	00701053 / $16.99	
VOL. 109 – STEVE MILLER	00701054 / $14.99	
VOL. 110 – SLIDE GUITAR HITS	00701055 / $16.99	
VOL. 111 – JOHN MELLENCAMP	00701056 / $14.99	
VOL. 112 – QUEEN	00701052 / $16.99	
VOL. 113 – JIM CROCE	00701058 / $15.99	
VOL. 114 – BON JOVI	00701060 / $14.99	
VOL. 115 – JOHNNY CASH	00701070 / $16.99	
VOL. 116 – THE VENTURES	00701124 / $14.99	
VOL. 117 – BRAD PAISLEY	00701224 / $16.99	
VOL. 118 – ERIC JOHNSON	00701353 / $16.99	
VOL. 119 – AC/DC CLASSICS	00701356 / $17.99	
VOL. 120 – PROGRESSIVE ROCK	00701457 / $14.99	
VOL. 121 – U2	00701508 / $16.99	
VOL. 122 – CROSBY, STILLS & NASH	00701610 / $16.99	
VOL. 123 – LENNON & MCCARTNEY ACOUSTIC	00701614 / $16.99	
VOL. 125 – JEFF BECK	00701687 / $16.99	
VOL. 126 – BOB MARLEY	00701701 / $16.99	
VOL. 127 – 1970S ROCK	00701739 / $14.99	
VOL. 128 – 1960S ROCK	00701740 / $16.99	

VOL. 129 – MEGADETH	00701741 / $16.99	
VOL. 131 – 1990S ROCK	00701743 / $14.99	
VOL. 132 – COUNTRY ROCK	00701757 / $15.99	
VOL. 133 – TAYLOR SWIFT	00701894 / $16.99	
VOL. 134 – AVENGED SEVENFOLD	00701906 / $16.99	
VOL. 136 – GUITAR THEMES	00701922 / $14.99	
VOL. 137 – IRISH TUNES	00701966 / $15.99	
VOL. 138 – BLUEGRASS CLASSICS	00701967 / $14.99	
VOL. 139 – GARY MOORE	00702370 / $16.99	
VOL. 140 – MORE STEVIE RAY VAUGHAN	00702396 / $17.99	
VOL. 141 – ACOUSTIC HITS	00702401 / $16.99	
VOL. 143 – SLASH	00702425 / $19.99	
VOL. 144 – DJANGO REINHARDT	00702531 / $16.99	
VOL. 145 – DEF LEPPARD	00702532 / $16.99	
VOL. 146 – ROBERT JOHNSON	00702533 / $16.99	
VOL. 147 – SIMON & GARFUNKEL	14041591 / $16.99	
VOL. 148 – BOB DYLAN	14041592 / $16.99	
VOL. 149 – AC/DC HITS	14041593 / $17.99	
VOL. 150 – ZAKK WYLDE	02501717 / $16.99	
VOL. 152 – JOE BONAMASSA	02501751 / $19.99	
VOL. 153 – RED HOT CHILI PEPPERS	00702990 / $19.99	
VOL. 155 – ERIC CLAPTON – FROM THE ALBUM UNPLUGGED	00703085 / $16.99	
VOL. 156 – SLAYER	00703770 / $17.99	
VOL. 157 – FLEETWOOD MAC	00101382 / $16.99	
VOL. 158 – ULTIMATE CHRISTMAS	00101889 / $14.99	
VOL. 159 – WES MONTGOMERY	00102593 / $19.99	
VOL. 160 – T-BONE WALKER	00102641 / $16.99	
VOL. 161 – THE EAGLES – ACOUSTIC	00102659 / $17.99	
VOL. 162 – THE EAGLES HITS	00102667 / $17.99	
VOL. 163 – PANTERA	00103036 / $17.99	
VOL. 164 – VAN HALEN 1986-1995	00110270 / $17.99	
VOL. 166 – MODERN BLUES	00700764 / $16.99	
VOL. 167 – DREAM THEATER	00111938 / $24.99	
VOL. 168 – KISS	00113421 / $16.99	
VOL. 169 – TAYLOR SWIFT	00115982 / $16.99	
VOL. 170 – THREE DAYS GRACE	00117337 / $16.99	
VOL. 171 – JAMES BROWN	00117420 / $16.99	
VOL. 172 – THE DOOBIE BROTHERS	00119670 / $16.99	
VOL. 174 – SCORPIONS	00122119 / $16.99	
VOL. 175 – MICHAEL SCHENKER	00122127 / $16.99	
VOL. 176 – BLUES BREAKERS WITH JOHN MAYALL & ERIC CLAPTON	00122132 / $19.99	
VOL. 177 – ALBERT KING	00123271 / $16.99	
VOL. 178 – JASON MRAZ	00124165 / $17.99	
VOL. 179 – RAMONES	00127073 / $16.99	
VOL. 180 – BRUNO MARS	00129706 / $16.99	
VOL. 181 – JACK JOHNSON	00129854 / $16.99	
VOL. 182 – SOUNDGARDEN	00138161 / $17.99	
VOL. 184 – KENNY WAYNE SHEPHERD	00138258 / $17.99	
VOL. 185 – JOE SATRIANI	00139457 / $17.99	
VOL. 186 – GRATEFUL DEAD	00139459 / $17.99	
VOL. 187 – JOHN DENVER	00140839 / $17.99	
VOL. 189 – JOHN MAYER	00144350 / $17.99	

Complete song lists available online.

Prices, contents, and availability subject to change without notice.

HAL•LEONARD®
CORPORATION

7777 W. BLUEMOUND RD. P.O. BOX 13819 MILWAUKEE, WI 53213

www.halleonard.com

0416

EASY GUITAR WITH NOTES & TAB

This series features simplified arrangements with notes, tab, chord charts, and strum and pick patterns.

MIXED FOLIOS

00702287	Acoustic	$14.99
00702002	Acoustic Rock Hits for Easy Guitar	$12.95
00702166	All-Time Best Guitar Collection	$19.99
00699665	Beatles Best	$12.95
00702232	Best Acoustic Songs for Easy Guitar	$12.99
00119835	Best Children's Songs	$16.99
00702233	Best Hard Rock Songs	$14.99
00703055	The Big Book of Nursery Rhymes & Children's Songs	$14.99
00322179	The Big Easy Book of Classic Rock Guitar	$24.95
00698978	Big Christmas Collection	$16.95
00702394	Bluegrass Songs for Easy Guitar	$12.99
00703387	Celtic Classics	$14.99
00142539	Chart Hits of 2014-2015	$14.99
00702149	Children's Christian Songbook	$7.95
00702237	Christian Acoustic Favorites	$12.95
00702028	Christmas Classics	$7.95
00101779	Christmas Guitar	$14.99
00702185	Christmas Hits	$9.95
00702141	Classic Rock	$8.95
00702203	CMT's 100 Greatest Country Songs	$27.95
00702283	The Contemporary Christian Collection	$16.99
00702239	Country Classics for Easy Guitar	$19.99
00702282	Country Hits of 2009–2010	$14.99

00702085	Disney Movie Hits	$12.95
00702257	Easy Acoustic Guitar Songs	$14.99
00702280	Easy Guitar Tab White Pages	$29.99
00702212	Essential Christmas	$9.95
00702041	Favorite Hymns for Easy Guitar	$9.95
00140841	4-Chord Hymns for Guitar	$7.99
00702281	4 Chord Rock	$9.99
00126894	Frozen	$14.99
00702286	Glee	$16.99
00699374	Gospel Favorites	$14.95
00122138	The Grammy Awards® Record of the Year 1958-2011	$19.99
00702160	The Great American Country Songbook	$15.99
00702050	Great Classical Themes for Easy Guitar	$6.95
00702116	Greatest Hymns for Guitar	$8.95
00702130	The Groovy Years	$9.95
00702184	Guitar Instrumentals	$9.95
00148030	Halloween Guitar Songs	$14.99
00702273	Irish Songs	$12.99
00702275	Jazz Favorites for Easy Guitar	$14.99
00702274	Jazz Standards for Easy Guitar	$14.99
00702162	Jumbo Easy Guitar Songbook	$19.95
00702258	Legends of Rock	$14.99
00702261	Modern Worship Hits	$14.99
00702189	MTV's 100 Greatest Pop Songs	$24.95
00702272	1950s Rock	$14.99

00702271	1960s Rock	$14.99
00702270	1970s Rock	$14.99
00702269	1980s Rock	$14.99
00702268	1990s Rock	$14.99
00109725	Once	$14.99
00702187	Selections from O Brother Where Art Thou?	$12.95
00702178	100 Songs for Kids	$14.99
00702515	Pirates of the Caribbean	$12.99
00702125	Praise and Worship for Guitar	$9.95
00702155	Rock Hits for Guitar	$9.95
00702285	Southern Rock Hits	$12.99
00702866	Theme Music	$12.99
00121535	30 Easy Celtic Guitar Solos	$14.99
00702220	Today's Country Hits	$9.95
00702198	Today's Hits for Guitar	$9.95
00121900	Today's Women of Pop & Rock	$14.99
00702217	Top Christian Hits	$12.95
00103626	Top Hits of 2012	$14.99
00702294	Top Worship Hits	$14.99
00702206	Very Best of Rock	$9.95
00702255	VH1's 100 Greatest Hard Rock Songs	$27.99
00702175	VH1's 100 Greatest Songs of Rock and Roll	$24.95
00702253	Wicked	$12.99

ARTIST COLLECTIONS

00702267	AC/DC for Easy Guitar	$15.99
00702598	Adele for Easy Guitar	$14.99
00702001	Best of Aerosmith	$16.95
00702040	Best of the Allman Brothers	$14.99
00702865	J.S. Bach for Easy Guitar	$12.99
00702169	Best of The Beach Boys	$12.99
00702292	The Beatles — 1	$19.99
00125796	Best of Chuck Berry	$14.99
00702201	The Essential Black Sabbath	$12.95
02501615	Zac Brown Band — The Foundation	$16.99
02501621	Zac Brown Band — You Get What You Give	$16.99
00702043	Best of Johnny Cash	$16.99
00702291	Very Best of Coldplay	$12.99
00702263	Best of Casting Crowns	$12.99
00702090	Eric Clapton's Best	$10.95
00702086	Eric Clapton — from the Album Unplugged	$10.95
00702202	The Essential Eric Clapton	$12.95
00702250	blink-182 — Greatest Hits	$12.99
00702053	Best of Patsy Cline	$10.95
00702229	The Very Best of Creedence Clearwater Revival	$14.99
00702145	Best of Jim Croce	$14.99
00702278	Crosby, Stills & Nash	$12.99
00702219	David Crowder*Band Collection	$12.95
14042809	Bob Dylan	$14.99
00702276	Fleetwood Mac — Easy Guitar Collection	$14.99
00130952	Foo Fighters	$14.99
00139462	The Very Best of Grateful Dead	$14.99
00702136	Best of Merle Haggard	$12.99
00702227	Jimi Hendrix — Smash Hits	$14.99
00702288	Best of Hillsong United	$12.99

00702236	Best of Antonio Carlos Jobim	$12.95
00702245	Elton John — Greatest Hits 1970–2002	$14.99
00129855	Jack Johnson	$14.99
00702204	Robert Johnson	$10.99
00702234	Selections from Toby Keith — 35 Biggest Hits	$12.95
00702003	Kiss	$9.95
00110578	Best of Kutless	$12.99
00702216	Lynyrd Skynyrd	$15.99
00702182	The Essential Bob Marley	$12.95
00146081	Maroon 5	$14.99
00702346	Bruno Mars — Doo-Wops & Hooligans	$12.99
00121925	Bruno Mars – Unorthodox Jukebox	$12.99
00702248	Paul McCartney — All the Best	$14.99
00702129	Songs of Sarah McLachlan	$12.95
00125484	The Best of MercyMe	$12.99
02501316	Metallica — Death Magnetic	$15.95
00702209	Steve Miller Band — Young Hearts (Greatest Hits)	$12.95
00124167	Jason Mraz	$14.99
00702096	Best of Nirvana	$14.99
00702211	The Offspring — Greatest Hits	$12.95
00138026	One Direction	$14.99
00702030	Best of Roy Orbison	$12.95
00702144	Best of Ozzy Osbourne	$14.99
00702279	Tom Petty	$12.99
00102911	Pink Floyd	$16.99
00702139	Elvis Country Favorites	$9.95
00702293	The Very Best of Prince	$12.99
00699415	Best of Queen for Guitar	$14.99
00109279	Best of R.E.M.	$14.99
00702208	Red Hot Chili Peppers — Greatest Hits	$12.95

00702093	Rolling Stones Collection	$17.95
00702196	Best of Bob Seger	$12.95
00146046	Ed Sheeran	$14.99
00702252	Frank Sinatra — Nothing But the Best	$12.99
00702010	Best of Rod Stewart	$14.95
00702049	Best of George Strait	$12.95
00702259	Taylor Swift for Easy Guitar	$14.99
00702260	Taylor Swift — Fearless	$12.99
00139727	Taylor Swift — 1989	$17.99
00115960	Taylor Swift — Red	$16.99
00702290	Taylor Swift — Speak Now	$15.99
00702262	Chris Tomlin Collection	$14.99
00702226	Chris Tomlin — See the Morning	$12.95
00148643	Train	$14.99
00702427	U2 — 18 Singles	$14.99
00102711	Van Halen	$16.99
00702108	Best of Stevie Ray Vaughan	$10.95
00702123	Best of Hank Williams	$12.99
00702111	Stevie Wonder — Guitar Collection	$9.95
00702228	Neil Young — Greatest Hits	$15.99
00119133	Neil Young — Harvest	$14.99
00702188	Essential ZZ Top	$10.95

Prices, contents and availability subject to change without notice.

7777 W. Bluemound Rd. P.O. Box 13819 Milwaukee, WI 53213

Visit Hal Leonard online at
www.halleonard.com

0316